SING A NEW SONG

Jim Prestidge

Bible passages are quoted from
The Revised English Bible
Cambridge University Press
and Oxford University Press

Gotham Books

30 N Gould St.
Ste. 20820, Sheridan, WY 82801
https://gothambooksinc.com/

Phone: 1 (307) 464-7800

© 2025 *Jim Prestidge*. All rights reserved.

No part of this book may be reproduced, stored in a retrieval system, or transmitted by any means without the written permission of the author.

Published by Gotham Books (April 23, 2025)

ISBN: 979-8-3484-9421-6 (P)
ISBN: 979-8-3484-9422-3 (E)

Because of the dynamic nature of the Internet, any web addresses or links contained in this book may have changed since publication and may no longer be valid.

The views expressed in this work are solely those of the author and do not necessarily reflect the views of the publisher, and the publisher hereby disclaims any responsibility for them.

CONTENTS

WHAT IS LIFE 1
EARTH'S POTENTIAL 3
    CHURCH 4
    MERCY PEACE AND TRUTH 5
    SATURDAY NIGHT 6
    MY GIFT TO GOD 7
WOUNDS 9
    WHY DID SHE DO THAT 9
    FROM JOHN 3:14-21 11
    JUSTICE 14
    MISTAKES 15
THE NEW LIFE 17
    IF 18
    THE BOOK OF LIFE 21
    GOD'S ANGELS 22
THE GREAT COMMANDMENT 27
FIND MYSELF 35
    NEW YEAR 36
    CREATE IN ME 37
    WHAT MAKES A DAY 41
    LORD OF EVERYTHING 43
A NEW WORLD 47
    PICTURES OF WAR 48
    TWO THOUSAND YEARS 51

WHAT IS LIFE

There is general consensus that the world should be better than it is. On the one hand we have so many things which make the daily tasks easier, our lives are getting longer. On the other hand we see things that are far from right. The hopes of the twentieth century have changed into suspicion, doubt and anxiety. Christians look to the Second Coming of Jesus to put it all right. Is it not in our hands to outlaw evil now? Are our present actions actually delaying the Second Coming?

> Up and down
> In and out
> Round about
> Goes the world
>
> Never stop
> Do not think
> Where it all
> Is leading
>
> Jesus said
> Follow me
> Live the life
> God gave you

Then he called the people to him, as well as his disciples, and said to them, 'Anyone who wants to be a follower of mine must renounce self; he must take up his cross and follow me. Whoever wants to save his life will lose it, but whoever loses his life for my sake and for the gospel's will save it. What does anyone gain by winning the whole world at the cost of his life? What can he give to buy his life back? (Mark 8:34–37)

EARTH'S POTENTIAL

Western countries have moved to a point where the welfare state has taken care of the well being of each one of us. In losing our worries and gaining security we have drifted into a dependence on the state and an expectation that the state will order our lives. We have lost our sense of responsibility. Our lives drift securely along, but we have lost control.

At the same time the media have assumed a controlling influence over our knowledge and thinking.

The welfare state has given us time and freedom, each one to make our personal contribution to a better life for all. Jesus showed us the way. We each need to seize that Higher Power and let it lead us. After all, God designed the world and made it according to his plan.

    I speak the truth,
    Tell out my mind,
    My considered opinion.

    The world goes round,
    Unthinkingly,
    Blathering on and on.

    People caught up,
    Fancy ideas,
    Living by the system.

    Will you join me?
    Make Earth a place
    informed, well run, happy.

Why do you call me "Lord, Lord"–and never do what I tell you? Everyone who comes to me and hears my words and acts on them–

I will show you what he is like. He is like a man building a house, who dug deep and laid the foundations on rock. When the river was in flood, it burst upon that house, but could not shift it, because it had been soundly built.
(Luke 6:46–48)

CHURCH

They go to church.
They say their prayers.
They go to work.
Forget their God.
No one thinks
that that is odd.

In the street.
Someone they know.
They share bad news.
The gossip too.
God waits to hear
good things and true.

They're short of cash.
An offer comes.
They snap it up.
And thank their luck.
They never say
what care God took.

Feeling tired and down.
Lonely too.
A friend drops in.
Their gloom to end.
No thanks to God
who sent the friend.

A walk in the country.
The air is so fresh.
They feast on the beauty.

They are looking at.
God made it all.
They don't say that.

We say to ourselves.
How much they miss.
We judge them bad.
We make a fuss.
We never think
that they are us.

We ask God that you may receive from him full insight into his will, all wisdom and spiritual understanding, so that your manner of life may be worthy of the Lord and entirely pleasing to him. We pray that you may bear fruit in active goodness of every kind, and grow in knowledge of God. In his glorious might may he give you ample strength to meet with fortitude and patience whatever comes; and to give joyful thanks to the Father who has made you fit to share the heritage of God's people in the realm of light.
(Colossians 1:9–12)

MERCY PEACE AND TRUTH
When we hear of justice
we hear vindictiveness,
we do not hear mercy.
When we hear the news
we do not hear peace.
When we hear the media
we hear contrived opinions.
We do not hear truth.

Mercy peace and truth
are God's gift to us,
to share with the world.
Mercy peace and truth.
We are the light of the world.
We are the salt of the world.
To awaken the world

to mercy peace and truth.

You are salt to the world. And if salt becomes tasteless, how is its saltness to be restored? It is good for nothing but to be thrown away and trodden underfoot.
You are light for all the world. A town that stands on a hill cannot be hidden.
(Matthew 5:13–14)

SATURDAY NIGHT
Its saturday night.
What's on the tele?
All watch together.
We mustn't miss.
On monday at work
everyone will be talking.
I mustn't be left out.

Alone in his study,
the minister works hard.
A table lamp illuminates
well thumbed commentaries.
His is a Bible-based church.
He must find a text
for each point he makes.

Down the road
a young person bustles
to find the lectionary readings
for church tomorrow.
Must think them over
before the service.
Go well prepared.

Somewhere else,
In a quiet corner,
burns a candle.

Hands clasped. Head bowed.
Lost in prayer.
On the table a Bible
lies open.

In another place,
A more expressive prayer.
Muttering in tongues.
Oh for christian television.
Not at some obscure hour.
They have christians there.
Lord, you do it.

Quietly in Heaven
God loves them all,
longs to add his blessing.
Would they come together.
Share their zeals.
Find the holy bond
that unites humanity.

In a word, accept one another as Christ accepted us, to the glory of God.
(Romans 15:7)

MY GIFT TO GOD
What can I give the Lord?
It has to be really big.
All the world is his.
What can I give him,
that is not his already?

What does God want or need?
Every little thing he made.
One big world his design.
All the things, he made
and put them together.

What does God really love?
He loves the world, the cosmos,
carefully designed,
the work of his hands.
That has to include me.

I will give him myself.
But he already owns me.
A sadness I am.
My life goes astray,
not what was meant to be.

A gift I cannot give.
Nothing to the Almighty.
Only what is his due,
an apology.
My gift, to repair myself.

WOUNDS

Most of us carry wounds, hurts through something said or done, or perhaps an unfortunate thing happened. It often was not meant. Nevertheless the memory remains with us, may be for years and years. When a person is jumpy or touchy or awkward we should think that there is something nagging at them inside. They may not have worked it out. Think of their rudeness as a cry for help. The world is full of things, large and small, which call for healing.

WHY DID SHE DO THAT
Why did she do that to me!
Nasty spiteful thing she is.
Does not know how to behave.
Wanted to hurt my feelings.
Well, she will not get anything from me.
I will show her.

I did not mean to explode like that.
She took it the wrong way.
I will not speak to her again.
She will know how to treat other people.
What I said is true.
Someone had to tell her.

My friend, my friend, said Jesus,
addressing the two of them.
You should not think that way.
Two wrongs do not make a right.
None is perfect, as you know.
Understand what true love is.

You do not know what was inside her

to make it happen like that.
You did not see her plight,
sensitive spots within.
You were ruled by feelings, nothing more.
I crucified them on the cross for both of you.

Hear the Holy Spirit behind you.
The still small voice guides aright.[1]
As God sees you, loves you,
you see, love each other.
Find the good that is there.
Uplift, never destroy.

Away with feelings, self-centredness.
Look always beyond yourself.
It takes two to quarrel.
Be you his child of peace.
Live the way of Jesus.
A bigger person be.

Friends, you must never speak ill of one another. He who speaks ill of a brother or passes judgement on him speaks ill of the law and judges the law. But if you judge the law, you are not keeping it but sitting in judgement upon it. There is only one lawgiver and judge: he who is able to save life or destroy it. So who are you to judge your neighbour?
(James 4:11-12)

Jesus teaches Truth. The Lie,
Satan's propaganda,
aims to destroy.
It put Jesus on the cross,
to rise again.

The Truth frees from all that,
puts wrong in perspective.

---

[1] 1 Kings 19:11–13

Not to be hurt.
Be sad for them, not you.
Satan exposed.

The serpent in Eden.
The craftiest of creatures.
We blame each other.
Become his victims.
To Hell with Satan.

Thanks be to God of Creation,
King of them and us.
On the victor's side we,
God's children of light,
light up the world.

Do not judge, and you will not be judged. For as you judge others, so you will yourselves be judged, and whatever measure you deal out to others will be dealt to you. Why do you look at the speck of sawdust in your brother's eye, with never a thought for the plank in your own?
(Matthew 7:1–3)

FROM JOHN 3:14-21
Eden, land of the river,
that branches into four.
Pleasant place, Earth's cradle.
The serpent had a plot.
The fruit, isn't it good!
You will not die, God knows
you will know good
and evil.
So came our mixed world.

Serpents in the dessert.
Venomous snakes, will we make it
to the Promised Land?
A serpent on a pole,

a serpent of bronze, lifeless.
Look at it, nothing can it do,
but heal, if with faith
one looks through it to God
the healer.

Pilate's praetorium.
Verdicts of not guilty.[2]
The serpent's voice was shrill.
Crucify![3]
Hang on a cross by the arms.
Naked.
O such cruel cruel pain.
The serpent victorious shines.
Or so they would believe.

Destroy this temple.
In three days from death to life
I will raise my body,
just a sabbath rest between.
Where is the serpent now?
Gone.
Gone from my life and yours.
Look up to the empty cross.
Believe Jesus. Follow him.

Sin, judgement, death,
the lake of eternal fire.
God's court decrees
it does not have to be.
He did not come to judge.
Jesus came to save,
to rescue,
to show another way,
for those who take it.

---

[2] Luke 23: 4, 14–15, 22
[3] Luke 23:20–21

And if you don't, where then?
The case stays open.
You the judge who decides it.
You turned away.
I know my way,
though it bring my end.
What do I care
I am master of my life.
Or am I?

Look to the empty cross,
to the one who hung there.
The pain and shame he called his glory.
Hear him.
Live by the Truth.
The light came to the world.
The Truth or the Lie you choose.
I made my choice.
He lives within my heart.

A Child of Light am I.
No hiding in dark corners.
That which he puts in me
goes out to all my neighbours.
Not I for me and me for myself.
The serpent's Lie that is.
God in me through me is the Truth.
In every thing I say or do,
his light for the world to see.

No one who puts his faith in him comes under judgement; but the unbeliever has already been judged because he has not put his trust in God's only Son. This is the judgement: the light has come into the world, but people preferred darkness to light because their deeds were evil. Wrongdoers hate the light and avoid it, for fear their misdeeds should be exposed. Those who live by the truth come to the light so that it may be clearly seen that God is in all they do. (John 3:18–21)

JUSTICE
He must be brought to justice.
I can't forgive a thing like that.
Look what it's done to me.
I demand an enquiry.

He did not mean.
Or if he did
he was misled.
He needs to be shown
a better way.

He can learn in prison.
That will balance what he did.
His long sentence
will put me right.

Mess up another life?
There is another way.
Reject the world's wrong ways.
You give him peace,
peace comes to you.

Love your enemy!
How could Jesus say a thing like that!
My friend, it's true.
Love and forgiveness heal.
The only medicine that works.

Father, may your name be hallowed;
your kingdom come.
Give us each day our daily bread.
And forgive us our sins,
for we too forgive all who have done us wrong.
And do not put us to the test.
(Luke 11:2–4)

MISTAKES
I should not have said it.
It seemed the right thing at the time.
I should have asked the Father.
Been guided by Him.

Pause, think before speaking.
Not words from you but from Him.
Words to calm down, sooth, bring peace.
Hurt not, rather heal.

Live at peace among yourselves. We urge you, friends, to rebuke the idle, encourage the faint-hearted, support the weak, and be patient with everyone.
See to it that no one pays back wrong for wrong, but always aim at what is best for each other and for all.
(1 Thessalonians 5:13–15)

O Lord and Father of us all,
of us as well as them,
You created them in your image,
as you created all the world
to live caringly together.

You sent us Jesus,
to teach the great principle of love.
Sin put him to death.
We let evil take control.
Push us to escape from the Evil One.

Bring us at last to our senses.
Push hard, 'til it really hurts.
To be your holy family,
your Kingdom here on Earth.

THE NEW LIFE

To live God's life made for us the destructive thinking that we have picked up has to be removed. We have to be 'born again', that is, our minds restarted. We were made in God's image. To fit that we need to see things God's way.
We think about other people and their wellbeing and the general good. We treat others as we would like them to treat us. If we love God he provides for us, we do not have to worry about ourselves.
Most people try to do what is right, but often we only know part of the story. Things go wrong, even between well meaning people. It happens both at personal and international levels. Jesus pointed us to a way out and on.
The teaching of Jesus heralded a new era, in which our ways become as they should be. Is that not what our hearts long for?

> God created a world
> beautifully made.
> To live in harmony.
> Evil wormed a way in.
>
> God sent his Son Jesus.
> Showed a better way.
> Brought us to our senses.
> Not all saw it like that.
>
> A mixture it became.
> Care, strife, bickering.
> Caught in evil's snare.
> We need to know the Lord.
>
> Follow me, said Jesus.
> Live the life of love.

Away with care and strife.
All change your ways and live.

Jesus answered, 'In very truth I tell you, no one can enter the kingdom of God without being born from water and spirit. Flesh can give birth only to flesh; it is spirit that gives birth to spirit.
(John 3:5–6)

As many as received him,
continued John,
to those he showed the how:
reborn to God's true way
by water and the Spirit.

Darkness holds us prisoner,
when we think we are so free.
Light of the world come to us.
Life of the Lord come to us.
Your true life fill us and bless.

A new perspective we get,
God's way of thinking.
That of confused man,
that which confused man,
all gone, we begin afresh.

Always treat others as you would like them to treat you: that is the law and the prophets.
(Matthew 7:12)

IF
If you love me,
said Jesus,
do all that I say to you.
I live in you and you in me,
for everyone to see
that you are my disciple,
directing God's love to them.

If you do in my name,
declared Jesus,
the things I give you to do,
the Father will love you.
So light the way for others.
Be true children of God,
pointing the world to his Kingdom.

If you follow my path,
promised Jesus,
I will send you the Holy Spirit.
He will lead and guide you,
remind you what I said.
You are salt and light to the world.
It all begins with if.

If you love me you will obey my commands; and I will ask the Father, and he will give you another to be your advocate, who will be with you for ever– the Spirit of truth. The world cannot accept him, because the world neither sees nor knows him; but you know him, because he dwells with you and will be in you.
(John 14:15–17)

Two stories Jesus told
about himself, his work
and God the Father.
How we fit together
to be his people.

The stories reveal to us
ourselves, our nature
to be at one together,
how we really belong
in the order of things.

I am the true vine Jesus said.[4]
You are branches, I the support.
I hold your leaves to the light,
bring water from the soil and nutrients.
You grow healthy, productive.

Farmer God he tends you.
He knows how a vine should be.
Each wrong move he prunes away.
If his care has no avail
into the fire you go.

I am your shepherd, Jesus said.[5]
I know my sheep, they know me.
I lead them along the way.
I have pastures prepared.
The Lord my shepherd is.

The Mediterranean shepherd
does not drive his sheep along
pushing them where to go.
Ahead he goes, he leads.
He calls, they hear, they follow.

Together the stories tell
of a purposeful existence.
A super-intelligence guides.
God keeps us together.
We are his pride, his very flock.

Do not ask anxiously, "What are we to eat? What are we to drink? What shall we wear?" These are the things that occupy the minds of the heathen, but your heavenly Father knows that you need them all. Set your mind on God's kingdom and his justice before everything else, and all the rest will come to you as well.

---

[4] John 15:1–10
[5] John 10:11–16

(Matthew 6:31–33)

> Louder still and clearly,
> God's song we sing.
> Jesus Christ our Saviour
> takes care of everything.

See to it that no one pays back wrong for wrong, but always aim at what is best for each other and for all.
Always be joyful; pray continually; give thanks whatever happens; for this is what God wills for you in Christ Jesus.
(1 Thessalonians 5:15–16)

> **THE BOOK OF LIFE**
> Africa has a saying,
> as many sayings there are:
> when an old person dies,
> it is like burning
> a library.
> Africa values old people.
>
> The library of your life,
> take care what goes in it.
> Only good books should it have,
> chosen and given
> by God himself.
> No rubbish, nothing of shame.
>
> The books that you are given,
> however many they be,
> every book, every page,
> a joy to reread,
> to remember.
> Open them up to your friends.
>
> When the last book is closed,
> the last chapter written,
> nothing to add or change,

> Good faithful servant,
> hear Jesus say.
> Memory of you lingers on.

Those of us who are strong must accept as our own burden the tender scruples of the weak, and not just please ourselves. Each of us must consider his neighbour and think what is for his good and will build up the common life. Christ too did not please himself...
(Romans 15:1–3)

> **GOD'S ANGELS**
> Let us be God's angels,
> carry messages from him,
> connect Him to others,
> speak a timely word in their ear,
> show what God's children can do.
> Children of Light are we,
> taught by Jesus himself,
> the way of the Lord to be.

If anyone is caught doing something wrong, you, my friends, who live by the Spirit must gently set him right. Look to yourself, each one of you: you also may be tempted. Carry one another's burdens, and in this way you will fulfil the law of Christ. (Galatians 6:1–2)

> I make a mistake.
> They put me right.
> Kindly, gently they do it.
> I am not demolished.
> They all work for my good.
> God's love pervades.
> It looks for an open door,
> to enter in and on.

But a Samaritan who was going that way came upon him, and when he saw him he was moved to pity. He went up and bandaged his wounds, bathing them with oil and wine. Then he lifted him on to

his own beast, brought him to an inn, and looked after him. Next day he produced two silver pieces and gave them to the innkeeper, and said, "Look after him; and if you spend more, I will repay you on my way back."
(Luke 10:33–35)

> **TODAY**
> Today, today.
> If today my soul is required of me,
> earthly joys and pleasures end,
> the planned conclusion of my life.
> Today to be with my Lord.
> His face to see.
> A new life to begin.
> Every day to be
> as it should have been before.

Greet one another with a loving kiss.
Peace to you all who belong to Christ.
(1 Peter 5:14)[6]

> When we meet
> how to start?
> Good morning?
> Hello there? Hi?
> Or go straight in?
> The greeting
> frames the meeting.
>
> Always start
> with a smile.
> It brings ease.
> Prepares the way.
> Ensures that
> all goes well.
> We make a mark.

---

[6] See also Romans 16:16, 1 Corinthians 16:20, 2 Corinthians 13:12

> With close friends,
> family,
> a kiss says
> unity.
> Togetherness.
> We belong.
> That's how we are.
>
> We Christians,
> together,
> filled with
> God in us,
> each other give
> happy smiles,
> a loving kiss.

Come, children, listen to me;
I shall teach you the fear of the Lord.
Which of you delights in life
and desires a long life to enjoy prosperity?
Then keep your tongue from evil
and your lips from telling lies;
shun evil and do good;
seek peace and pursue it.
The eyes of the Lord are on the righteous;
his ears are open to their cry.
(Psalm 34:11–15)

> The Lord's eyes are upon us,[7]
> see what we need and do.
> See which way we look, think and go.
> We gladden or sadden.
>
> Always speak truth, said Jesus,

---

[7] Proverbs chapter 15

words that uplift and console.
Consider the good of others.
They are God's children too.

Tell out the truth of Jesus
for all the world to know.
Seek first his Kingdom.
Truth, love, peace on earth.

Where are you going? asked Thomas.
He wanted to follow on.[8]
I am the way, said Jesus,
the Truth that leads to life.

Whatsoever things are true,
wrote Saint Paul in his letter.
Hold them in your mind.
So know his wonderful peace.

Always be true to others.
Be true to God and his word.
Walk humbly before him.
What more does God ask?

---

[8] John 14:5–6

THE GREAT COMMANDMENT

The great commandment of Jesus was to love. Love respects, cares for, understands the other, wants the best for them. That kind of love builds people up, brings them together.
Between a couple love is 'You love me, I love you'. In a group love is 'I love everybody, each loves the rest, everybody loves me'. Love flows through us and out and on into the world around. Communities and nations come together.
Love stems from God. Jesus' teaching raised judaism from a religion with rules for proper living into a way of life. The words of Jesus make the world a superb place to belong, if we do them.

      Love, love.
      What is love?
      Love that makes the world
      go round and round,
      brings a smile, raises spirits,
      a warm feeling, uplifts, releases,
      brings you and me together.

      Love, love.
      What is love?
      God's love for me.
      I feel a great contentment,
      protected, safe, upheld
      in the almighty arms.
      I am loved by Him.

      Love, love.
      What is love?
      Love my neighbour.
      Their lack, sorrow I dispel.

Wanted they feel, secure.
Our thoughts, our joys we share..
Tue friends we are.

Love, love.
What is love?
I love you. You love others.
They love all around them.
So love spreads ever outward,
encircling all the world,
and back to me.

It is not love
but loving
that makes the world go round.
An attitude from God.
Be it, think it, live it, do it.
Loving comes out in deeds.
Love in action.

A lawyer once came forward to test him by asking: 'Teacher, what must I do to inherit eternal life?' Jesus said, 'What is written in the law? What is your reading of it?' He replied, 'Love the Lord your God with all your heart, and with all your soul, with all your strength, and with all your mind; and your neighbour as yourself.' 'That is the right answer,' said Jesus; 'do that and you will have life.' (Luke 10:25–28)

A lawyer questioned Jesus.
Jesus turned the question back
on him to answer.
He was the expert, trained,
studied to know in detail
the Law they had from God.

Jesus did not come to change it.

> For ever stood the Law.[9]
> The expert stated it.
> Love God above all other.
> Love your neighbour as yourself.
> Correct, said Jesus, do it.

You, my friends, were called to be free; only beware of turning your freedom into licence for your unspiritual nature. Instead, serve one another in love; for the whole law is summed up in a single commandment: 'Love your neighbour as yourself.' But if you go on fighting one another, tooth and nail, all you can expect is mutual destruction.
(Galatians 5:13–15)

> Love your neighbour, Jesus said.
> Love yourself no more, no less.[10]
> Do as you would be done by.[11]
> True life all hangs on that.
>
> Who is my neighbour? the man asked.
> It has to be everyone.
> Anyone who comes near me.
> My close friend, of course.
> The stranger brushed by in the street.

But the harvest of the Spirit is love, joy, peace, patience, kindness, goodness, fidelity, gentleness, and self-control. Against such things there is no law.
(Galatians 5:22–23)

> We are all different.
> Some things they do annoy
> They disagree with me,
> question things I say and do.

---

[9] Matthew 5:17–18
[10] Matthew 22:39, Mark 12:31, Luke 10:27
[11] Matthew 7:12

> We are a mixed up family,
> brought up in different ways.
>
> One says something hurtful.
> They don't know how to love.
> God knows their need.
> His love in me shows me
> not to judge or be offended.
> Instead help, forgive, pray.
>
> Love all of them, said Jesus.
> Love is not to agree.
> The Devil, alert,
> puts in his foot where he can.[12]
> Love hates the action, the words said.
> Love fixes on the person.
>
> With God's help I can.
> Only with him inside me.
> His command, his wish
> build me to be like him.
> In every nasty disruptive thing
> I see a way out and on.

We who are mature should keep to this way of thinking. If on any point you think differently, this also God will make plain to you. Only let our conduct be consistent with what we have already attained.
(Philippians 3:13–16)

> I can never like him,
> doing the things he does.
> Nor can the Lord,
> said Jesus,
> clouded in sadness.
> He needs to be born again.

---

[12] 1 Peter 5:8-9

Show him the way to go,
the true way through life.

To love is not to like.
To love is not to approve.
Love wants the best for him.
Must bury my feelings.
It is my task to do.
He cannot change himself.
He has to know the Lord,
embrace his way.

To love the Lord
is the great commandment.
The second is like it:
love my neighbour.
I must be sure
that I am loveable too.
Jesus is the way the truth,
the life that is to be.

Love in all sincerity, loathing evil and holding fast to the good. Let love of the Christian community show itself in mutual affection. Esteem others more highly than yourself.
(Romans 12:9–10)

As I read the Bible
I hear Jesus say
Those who love me truly
do every word I say.[13]
What was Jesus telling me?

I had to love Jesus.
Surely that I did.
He is so good to me.
What was from me hid?

---

[13] John 14:15

My thoughts began to turn from me.
True love works two ways.
Not always receiving.
Be a light, He says.

He wanted me not as a pet.
A servant helper I should be.
Work for him, with him, through him.
He builds the world through me.

For all the world to see,
not how much He could bless,
though that was very great.
It was but only half or less.

Not to me, but through me.
His love to others had to flow.
Be the vehicle was my joy,
the way He would have me go.

God's love was for the world.
I am such a little bit.
The world has gone wrong.
My part God's hand to mend it.

How marvellous is God's love.
His wisdom it raised me high.
A noble purpose to achieve.
Sow love to make his Kingdom.

Do not judge, and you will not be judged; do not condemn, and you will not be condemned; pardon, and you will be pardoned; give, and gifts will be given you. Good measure, pressed and shaken down and running over, will be poured into your lap; for whatever measure you deal out to others will be dealt to you in turn.
(Luke 6:37–38)

It gives me a good feeling
to know that God loves me.
I feel safely guided.
He knows me through and through.
What does Jesus say to that?

Love is not a feeling.
Agape[14] love cares.
I have to go out of my way.
Do my all, give my all.
Easily said, then forgotten.

Jesus gave his all, his life.
Nothing less will do for me.
I keep my eyes open.
I notice others, I read their faces.
I put them on my donkey,
walk myself.
I foot the bill.
I go back to check, to do more.[15]

God's love within me does it.
I receive so as to give.
His love flows through me.
I am just the pipe.
With no kinks in it.
God is the great I Am.[16]
To do is my daily joy.

God's gift to me is giving.
I have them blessed, not me.
By God's good grace
all and more comes back to me.

---

[14] The highest of the four words for love in ancient greek
[15] The parable of The Good Samaritan: Luke 10:25–37
[16] The name of God; Exodus 3:13–15 See also the 'I am' statements of Jesus

FIND MYSELF

God created human beings to be like him: loving caring, considerate, in fact, what we call the christian virtues. We were to be together, under God. We have wandered very far from that. Our lives have deteriorated.
Jesus began his ministry with the Beatitudes or Blessings. Each is in two parts: the blessing and the consequence. They seem all upside down. In reality it is our lives that are upside down. The Beatitudes were Jesus' manifesto, how his teaching will put us right. They point us to think in another way, escape from what life has taught us.

Blessed are the poor in spirit;
the kingdom of Heaven is theirs.
Blessed are the sorrowful;
they shall find consolation.
Blessed are the gentle;
they shall have the earth for their possession.
Blessed are those who hunger and thirst to see right prevail;
they shall be satisfied.
Blessed are those who show mercy;
mercy shall be shown to them.
Blessed are those whose hearts are pure;
they shall see God.
Blessed are the peacemakers;
they shall be called God's children.
Blessed are those who are persecuted in the cause of right;
the kingdom of Heaven is theirs.
(Matthew 5:3–10)

NEW YEAR
Long long ago, in days gone by,
we made new year resolutions.
We sought our faults ourselves to improve.
A new year, a new start. Yes.
But did we keep it up - oh no!
Soon human nature took over.

Those days have long long gone.
Like the distant days of childhood.
Where is the new year of new hope?
We are modern and grown up.
Our lives controlled by what,
to a future that does not bear thinking.

Those long days of long ago,
filled up with childlike innocence,
seem now like a dream untrue.
Our resolutions were for ourself.
Ourself to improve, not our lives.
The world left to be as it is.

We long for the life of long ago.
We can't go back and get it.
Nor can we our future plan.
That's taken from our hands.
In what can we put our trust,
in this age of ease and pleasure?

Long long ago Jesus took a child,
stood him up before them.[17]
Except you return to those days, he said.
Those were the days of our innocence.
But then we grew to adults,
drinking in the good and the bad.

It was not such a long story,

---

[17] Matthew 18:1--5

> that Jesus told them long ago.
> And still it holds true today.
> Take the hand of God your maker.
> Make his mind and thoughts your own.
> So will your true life come.

God created human beings in his own image;
in the image of God he created them;
male and female he created them.
(Genesis 1:27)

> Come, Lord Jesus.
> Take the load off my back,
> the blinkers off my eyes,
> the shackles off my feet,
> the anaesthetic from my brain.
> Lord, show me myself.
> Bring out the real me,
> All that I long to be.

The Lord has told you mortals what is good,
and what it is that the Lord requires of you:
only to act justly, to love mercy,
to walk humbly with your God.
(Micah 6:8)

> **CREATE IN ME**
> She was so very nice.
> It always was a joy to be
> there in her company.
> One felt somehow uplifted,
> just to be in her presence.
> She made each occasion special.
>
> Her face was not that much
> to make one look twice at it.
> Yet people were drawn to her

by something there within.
One's own good feelings surged.
She roused the best in you and me.

Her eyes were quiet, not flashing.
They seemed to see into me.
Only good things they saw.
Things I hardly saw myself
stirred deep within me.
My inner self woke up, surfaced.

Inconspicuous was he.
Clothes like anyone wore.
A body inside them.
His voice no different from another.
His words, humble too,
inspired deep thoughts in others.

His was an inner wisdom
which must have come from God.
Natural not forced.
One did not feel inferior
alongside the gems he had.
Gems sparkled in you.

He noticed little problems
that other people had.
Quietly came a word,
appropriate, consoling.
Followed by a simple deed.
The difficulty shrunk and vanished.

What words have I to describe
what made her and him to be
as they clearly were.
Write a whole study book
to emulate better myself.
But their manner says it all.

> Dear Lord, dig out from me
> the things that you created,
> your gifts special to me,
> lovingly given to be used,
> your own image in me.
> Why ever did I neglect them.

Be known to everyone for your consideration of others.
The Lord is near; do not be anxious, but in everything make your requests known to God in prayer and petition with thanksgiving. Then the peace of God, which is beyond all understanding, will guard your hearts and your thoughts in Christ Jesus.
And now, my friends, all that is true, all that is noble, all that is just and pure, all that is lovable and attractive, whatever is excellent and admirable–fill your thoughts with these things.
(Philippians 4:5–8)

> In him was life,
> John begins his Gospel,
> pointing to Jesus,
> telling who he was:
> God's light for mankind.

> You are light for the world.
> Jesus turns the spotlight
> from himself to me.
> A city built on a hill
> cannot be hid.[18]

> Those who live by the Truth,
> wrote John again,
> come to the light
> for all the world to see
> Jesus' light through me.

---

[18] Matthew 5:14–16

You must work out your own salvation in fear and trembling; for it is God who works in you, inspiring both the will and the deed, for his own chosen purpose.
Do everything without grumbling or argument. Show yourselves innocent and above reproach, faultless children of God in a crooked and depraved generation, in which you shine like stars in a dark world and proffer the word of life.
(Philippians 2:12–16)

    Dear sister, brother, hear
    God's gentle voice calling.
    Be what he made you to be.
    Emerge, be your true self.
    The call is directed to you.
    Down tools, move on.
    There is a moment for all things,
    so the Preacher said.[19]
    This moment is yours.

    The rulers stood by the Law.
    Jesus did not change it.
    I come to complete, said He.[20]
    Jesus promised God's Holy Spirit.
    Our God is a consuming fire[21],
    Flames to empower or destroy,
    not to change our true nature.
    In God's image we were made.
    We need completing.

    Sister, brother dear.
    Open your life right now.
    Unpack what it really is.
    Complete what my words fail to say.

---

[19] Ecclesiastes 3:1–8
[20] Matthew 5:17
[21] Psalm 50:1–6

The Flame[22] hovers near.
Let it descend and stay.
This very moment to begin
your real life in Him.
Enter eternity.

Renouncing your former way of life, you must lay aside the old human nature which, deluded by its desires, is in process of decay: you must be renewed in mind and spirit, and put on the new nature created in God's likeness, which shows itself in the upright and devout life called for by the truth.
Then have done with falsehood and speak the truth to each other, for we belong to one another as parts of one body.
(Ephesians 4:22–24)

WHAT MAKES A DAY
What makes a day?
What makes a day go well?
What smooths the ups and downs?
What brings good decisions,
satisfaction at a day well spent?

What makes a task?
What makes a task go smoothly?
What directs it carrying through?
What steadies the workman's hand,
contentment at a job well done?

What makes a person?
What makes one happy, fulfilled?
What fills the mind with goodness?
What takes knocks and scrapes away,
letting the good prevail?

What makes my life?
What makes my life one joy?

---

[22] Acts 2:3–4

> What controls my actions?
> What makes me nice to others ,
> the Lord's way to show?
>
> Not by power, says the Lord,
> are good things achieved.
> Not by force, says the Lord,
> are others won over.
> Not by strength, says the Lord,
> are mountains moved,
> but by my Spirit,
> says the Lord of hosts.

For it is by grace you are saved through faith; it is not your own doing. It is God's gift, not a reward for work done. There is nothing for anyone to boast of; we are God's handiwork, created in Christ Jesus for the life of good deeds which God designed for us. (Ephesians 2:8–10)

> The love of God is marvellous.
> It fills me all the day.
> It colours all my doings,
> as I go on my way.
>
> A loving God understands me,
> knows all my weaknesses.
> Each time of doubt or stress
> He rushes in and blesses.
>
> My life has been transformed.
> Since I came in him to trust
> I go in confidence, not dread.
> To keep with him I must.

At that time the disciples came to Jesus and asked, 'Who is the greatest in the kingdom of Heaven?' He called a child, set him in front of them, and said, 'Truly I tell you: unless you turn round and become like children, you will never enter the kingdom of Heaven.

Whoever humbles himself and becomes like this child will be the greatest in the kingdom of Heaven, and whoever receives one such child in my name receives me. But if anyone causes the downfall of one of these little ones who believe in me, it would be better for him to have a millstone hung round his neck and be drowned in the depths of the sea.
(Matthew 18:1–6)

LORD OF EVERYTHING
Lord of all creation,
Your holy name we praise.
In all things to follow you
throughout all our days.

Lord of power and blessing,
gifts on us you pour.
Enable us to serve you.
Joyful be our life.

Lord of good relations,
as Jesus taught should be.
Enter every closed heart.
We live at peace through you.

Lord of strength and healing,
keep us to your way.
Alert and healthy people.
Responsive to your say.

Lord of time and hurry,
organise us, reprieve.
Compose our days aright.
We notice, act, achieve.

Lord of truth and beauty,
all good things start in you.
Flowers spring up around us.
Peace without within.

Lord of understanding,
intelligence and sight,
your mind flows out through us,
in your light delight.

May God himself, the God of peace, make you holy through and through, and keep you sound in spirit, soul, and body, free of any fault when our Lord Jesus Christ comes. He who calls you keeps faith; he will do it.
(1 Thessalonians 5:23–24)

Sister, brother, fill your heart,
your mind, your head, your thinking, doing
with all the things that Jesus taught,
to make us one in God.

Jesus, the way, the truth, the light.
In God's way, to be, to progress.
Happy, honest, fruitful, lives fulfilled.
As only God can do.

Love your neighbour, help, forgive.
Forget their silly ways, bless them instead.
Try it, see what comes back to you.
Away with care, trust God.

Human life is not existing,
Getting through it, then gone.
Service, caring, love, to give and get.
Go out of your way to do it.

Days chasing things that do not come.
No time for the Lord of Heaven.
Man needs an external being,
to truly guide us through.

Sister, brother, take the heeding.

Good places, joys, things accomplished.
End your time on earth with no regrets.
They all saw God in you.

A NEW WORLD

Thinking people realise that we are one world; we depend on each other. However, we go our own ways.
Fixed ideas, mistrust and suspicion keep people and nations apart. Self centered and shallow thinking dominates politics and economics. Doctrines influence understanding the Bible. People blame each other. Really most problems are self-generated. Conditions differ enormously across the world. Affluent countries have more than enough. They are little informed about the others, or even their neighbours. They think and act as if they were the world.

How far is it to heaven?
Too far to walk in a day.
Gone are youth's day dreams.
All blown away.

Study how to get there.
Our meetings lead the way.
Join the latest courses,
We have a full array.

People look no more to God.
The world has gone astray.
Isolate yourself.
Join with us we pray.

Love joy and peace,
did you hear Jesus say?
Listen for the inner call.
I am the truth, the life, the way.

> Open your mind to Jesus.
> Do what he says each day.
> Heaven is round the corner.
> Why not embrace it today?

I have delivered your word to them, and the world hates them because they are strangers in the world, as I am. I do not pray you to take them out of the world, but to keep them from the evil one. They are strangers in the world, as I am. Consecrate them by the truth; your word is truth. As you sent me into the world, I have sent them into the world...[23]
(John 17:14–18)

PICTURES OF WAR
Daughter, mother, father, son,
Sister, brother, husband, wife.
All dead and gone.
Or trapped in the rubble.
Unable to move.
They wait for death
to release them.
And I all alone. No job.
No money. Shops have gone.
No water in the tap.
How long can I last?
How many days or hours?
What will my body feel
as slowly it stops working?

A bullet hit me somewhere.
I can only lie as I am.
Or else the house fell down.
My home my safe haven.
Jagged broken masonry cuts
digs into my flesh.
The pain goes on and on.

---

[23] Jesus prays to his Father for us

Nothing can I do to ease it
How many hours or days?
Long cold nights, wet days.
Until pain fades away,
hope, longing, thought itself
no longer are.
Blessed are those who die quickly.

I am a soldier.
I am trained to obey, not to think.
The officer comes. I salute.
He gives the order.
I the machine to do it.
The general directs it all.
He has his instructions too
My fellow privates
pray for a small wound
to get out of what we are for.
The enemy does the same.
Would the pain of a wound,
perhaps be disabled for life,
be better than doing my job?

We need to be prepared.
We must have the best weapons.
Keep improving them.
They must be better than everyone else's.
Then we will win.
X may attack us.
If not X then Y.
We try to be friends.
We cannot trust them.
They spy on us.
Not a good sign.
Our intelligence is on the alert.
We want peaceful coexistence.
So we build for a bloody fight.

A voice cries:
'Clear a road through the wilderness for the Lord,
prepare a highway across the desert for our God.
Let every valley be raised,
every mountain and hill be brought low,
uneven ground be made smooth,
and steep places become level.
Then will the glory of the Lord be revealed
and all mankind together will see it.
The Lord himself has spoken.'
(Isaiah 40:3–5)[24]

    There are only two principles,
    as Jesus came to tell:
    God's Truth and Satan's Lie.
    Truth shines clear, illuminates.
    The Lie muddies it all up,
    doubts, confusion, sorrow brings.
    Shadows and darkness enter in
    to complicate God's good creation.
    Evil obscures the Light, the good.
    Good people go astray.
    The Lie has done its stuff, to make
    a world of troubles.

    Prisoners we all are held
    by the power the Lie has won.
    The Holy Spirit hovers over
    our chaos, as in the Creation[25],
    order to restore, God's free gift of Truth,
    stolen by the Lie.
    The Spirit opened the prison doors to Peter,[26]
    led him out to fresh healthy air.
    We know we should go, defy the Lie

---

[24] Quoted in Luke 3:4–6
[25] Genesis 1:1–3
[26] Acts 12:5–11

Only its creator holds us back.
Why leave space for that one,
we know is evil through and through?

Sister, brother dear,
open your heart, mind, soul, your all
to the Truth, as Jesus said.
Be done with all delusion.
Spring clean every forgotten corner.
Put the Lie in the rubbish bin.
Take on God's straight forward life.
Be a true child of Him.
All around will see
his truth in you, through you,
to re-create the world anew,
only Truth to be.

To eat and drink and experience pleasure in return for his labours, this does not come from any good in a person: it comes from God. For without God who can eat with enjoyment? He gives wisdom and knowledge and joy to whosoever is pleasing to him, while to the one who fails to please him is given the task of gathering and amassing wealth only to hand it over to someone else who does please God. This too is futility and a chasing of the wind.
(Ecclesiastes 2:24–26)

TWO THOUSAND YEARS
Jesus said to his Father,
Will they never learn.
To them I have been telling
the truth about your love.
Love is not just a feeling
to make each one feel good.
They have to love each other.

The Father said to his Son,
Two thousand years you have been telling
the truth about my love.

> Two thousand years is but a day.[27]
> Tomorrow has to come.

Set your troubled hearts at rest. Trust in God always; trust also in me. There are many dwelling-places in my Father's house; if it were not so I should have told you; for I am going to prepare a place for you.
(John 14:1–2)

> In my Father's house,
> so Jesus said,
> are many mansions.
> How can it be?
> A house is small.
> A mansion contains
> a great collection
> of most precious furnishings,
> the smallest of great value.
>
> Contradictory things
> Jesus was good at saying,
> to shake sleepy heads
> into reality.
> Thoughts, carelessly put together,
> He ruthlessly turns out.
> Replaces with great treasures.
> Each open mind he makes a mansion,
> full of God's precious things.

Be on your way; I am sending you like lambs among wolves. Carry no purse or pack, and travel barefoot. Exchange no greetings on the road. When you go into a house, let your first words be, "Peace to this house." If there is a man of peace there, your peace will rest on him; if not, it will return to you. (Luke 10:3–6)

> When you visit a house,

---
[27] Psalm 90:4

say peace on the house.
A person of peace, Jesus said,
will receive your peace.
Your visit leaves
its gift. Away you go.
God's peace stays there with them.

The peace which comes from God
is a gift to spread.
It surpasses understanding.[28]
Time, troubles, stand still.
We truly live.
The world fades away.
We seem in eternity.

Blessed are peacemakers.[29]
God's way seen in them.
They bring his peace to all the world.
They shall be called
God's children,
showing us their home
with God, in his Kingdom.

Prove yourselves at home in the light, for where light is, there is a harvest of goodness, righteousness, and truth. (Ephesians 5:8–9)

Not a world of believers yet was it,
built on Jesus' instructions to do.
Love God, love your neighbour, that's it.
Caring for all the others, them caring for you.

God first, self last, was the secret.
Eternal life, a community never to end.
A secret everyone knew and kept to.
God's wisdom conflict to mend.

---

[28] Philippians 4:5–8
[29] Matthew 5:9

Jesus gave us instructions to start it.
Then into our hearts it came.
Our awkward corners rubbed off.
Misfits somehow fitted the frame.

It was a vision of God's glory around us.
The Garden of Eden restored.[30]
Joy, peace and contentment fulfilling us.
One world, one people, one Lord.

Take another look at the scriptures.
It is there for us all to see.
Jesus opened the depths of God's mind.
So now let us think like He.

Praise to the Lord the Almighty,
for showing me where I went wrong.
May He heal the harm I did others,
when I thought I was singing his song.

For just as in a single human body there are many limbs and organs, all with different functions, so we who are united with Christ, though many, form one body, and belong to one another as its limbs and organs.
Let us use the different gifts allotted to each of us by God's grace…
(Romans 12:4–6)

Praise to the Lord.
His name lift high.
He is the King
of Creation.
Some dance and sing.
Some stand for Him.
Some kneel, head bowed,
eyes closed, silent.

---

[30] Genesis 2:8, 15 Genesis 3:23

He is their Lord.
And mine.

Listen to Him.
Small voice within.
Catch every word.
Then you do it.
Our God is love.
His love we give
to all around.
One we become.
He is my God.
And theirs.

You will recognize them by their fruit. Can grapes be picked from briars, or figs from thistles? A good tree always yields sound fruit, and a poor tree bad fruit. A good tree cannot bear bad fruit, or a poor tree sound fruit. A tree that does not yield sound fruit is cut down and thrown on the fire.
(Matthew 7:16–19)

The small voice spoke again to me.
'Take my love into the world.'
In half this world the nations
are in blocks, working together,
to get advantages from each other,
insincere words, nothing of love.
Occasionally a token remembrance
of the other half world, quietly waiting.

Said the voice in my head,
a still small voice, not nagging,
'Let each nation love each other,
be a united family,
with a loving Father,
sharing what each one has,
benefiting from each other.'
One world, one aim, one life, one God.

Scripture speaks of 'things beyond our seeing, things beyond our hearing, things beyond our imagining, all prepared by God for those who love him'; and these are what God has revealed to us through the Spirit. For the Spirit explores everything, even the depths of God's own nature. Who knows what a human being is but the human spirit within him? In the same way, only the Spirit of God knows what God is. And we have received this Spirit from God, not the spirit of the world, so that we may know all that God has lavished on us; and, because we are interpreting spiritual truths to those who have the Spirit, we speak of these gifts of God in words taught us not by our human wisdom but by the Spirit.
(1 Corinthians 2: 9–13)

>
> Praise, my soul, the King of Heaven.
> To the world new life he brings.
> Joy, purpose, proper working.
> Together, equal, one in Him.
>
> God is calling his people, come.
> Give planet Earth back to Him.
> Come, His chosen ones, with me.
> With one voice his new song to sing.

www.ingramcontent.com/pod-product-compliance
Lightning Source LLC
LaVergne TN
LVHW010617070526
838199LV00063BA/5172